LET'S FIND OUT

CATS

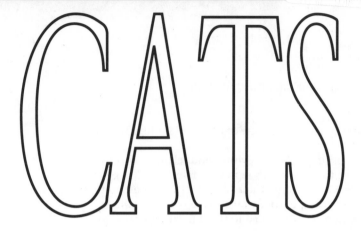

BARBARA HEHNER

Random House
Toronto

To Amanda Susan, with love

Published in Canada in 1990 by Random House of Canada Limited, Toronto.

All inquiries regarding the motion picture, television and related rights for
this book should be addressed to the author's representative, M.G.A. Agency
Inc., 10 St. Mary Street, Suite 510, Toronto, Canada M4Y 1P9. Representations
as to the disposition of these rights are strictly prohibited without express
written consent and will be vigorously pursued to the full extent of the law.

Canadian Cataloguing in Publication Data

Hehner, Barbara
  Let's find out about cats

ISBN 0-394-22087-0

1. Cats - Juvenile literature.   I. Title.

SF445.7.H43 1990   j636.8   C90-093171-X

COVER AND TEXT DESIGN: Brant Cowie/ArtPlus Limited
PAGE MAKE UP: Heather Brunton/ArtPlus Limited
TYPE OUTPUT: TypeLine Express Limited
ILLUSTRATIONS: Janet Wilson
COVER PHOTO: Superstock/Four by Five

Printed and bound in Canada

Contents

SECTION 1

Pawprints Through Time

Starting from Scratch

Which animal do you think makes a better pet, a cat or a dog? People have been arguing about this for a long, long time. Dog lovers think that their pets are friendlier and smarter. Cats, they say, are haughty, sneaky and cruel. Cat lovers consider their pets tidier, more graceful, and more dignified. Dogs, they say, are too messy, too noisy, and too eager to please.

Most of these people would be very surprised to find out that cats and dogs developed from the same long-ago animal. This animal was *Miacis*, a small, weasel-like mammal who lived 40 million years ago. Mammals are hairy or furry animals that feed milk to their babies. There are still lots of mammals around today. In fact, human beings are mammals.

Mammals first appeared about 200 million years ago, in the age of the dinosaurs. By the time Miacis came along, though, the dinosaurs were long gone. And Miacis was something new — a strong, fierce little mammal that killed other animals for food. Up to that time, all mammals were plant eaters. Miacis was the first *carnivore* (meat-eating mammal). Over millions of years, the Miacis family tree split into many branches. All of today's carnivores, including seals, bears, raccoons, weasels — and the dog and cat families — can trace their origins back to Miacis.

Animals that looked like the cats of today first appeared about 13 million years ago. We can tell from fossils — the bones these ancient cats left behind — that they were quite small, just a little bigger than modern house cats. It took 10 million more years before there were any big cats like today's lions and tigers.

When the earliest humanlike beings were beginning to walk upright and make tools (about one million years ago),

they had to watch out for the largest, fiercest cat that ever prowled the earth. This was *Smilodon*, the sabre-toothed tiger. Smilodon was heavier and stronger than today's lions and tigers. It had huge, sharp eyeteeth, 20 cm (8 inches) long, to stab its prey. Aren't you relieved that the last sabre-toothed tiger died about 10,000 years ago?

Ten thousand years ago, human beings were beginning to grow plants for food. They were also raising cattle and goats. These people made fires to keep warm and cook their food, and their faithful dogs slept around their campfires with them. People may have seen cats gliding in the shadows, their eyes glowing in the firelight. But cats were

3

probably too wary to come any closer. Many dog bones have been found in these early settlements, but no cat bones. Not a single cat is shown in the cave wall paintings that these people left behind.

We really don't know how cats first moved in with human beings. One good guess is that people met cats when they began to farm. When people sowed seeds, birds and mice came to eat them. And what stalked the birds and mice? Cats, of course. Maybe, at first, people let cats live near their homes, half-wild and half-tame, because it was good for their crops. But at some point a child may have cuddled a kitten and brought it inside. Or maybe a cat sidled up to the fire, crept into someone's lap, and purred while it was stroked.

We don't know exactly when this happened. We do know that, by about 4,000 years ago, the cats in ancient Egypt were loved and prized above any other animal. But that's another story.

SOMETHING TO SEND FOR

CATNIP DELIGHT

Many cats are thrilled by the smell and taste of a plant called catnip. They sniff it, chew it, and roll over in it. Even very dignified cats often frisk and pounce like kittens.

You can grow catnip from seed in your own garden or even in a window box. A seed company in Alberta will send you four packets of catnip seeds with a clear explanation of how to plant them. Along with the seeds, you will also receive a 26-page gardening activity booklet, which has pictures to color and trace, puzzles and easy experiments.

Write to:
Alberta Nurseries and Seeds Ltd., Dept. C
Bowden Alberta,
TOM OKO

Ask for: 4 packets of catnip seeds and Garden Kids Family activity book.

Cost: $2.00

Don't forget: Print your own address clearly on your letter, so that they'll know where to send your seeds.

The First Pussycats?

What kinds of cats were the first ones to be tamed? Nobody knows for sure, but there are some good guesses from people who study cats. Many of them think that the African wild cat, *Felis lybica*, was the ancestor of today's pet cats. It lives in the part of the world where we first know of tame cats — in the Middle East and North Africa. The African wild cat doesn't look much different from domestic cats. It's a little bigger — about 4.5 to 8 kg (10 to 18 lbs.) — and it's usually brown or golden yellow, sometimes with faint stripes. It's an easy cat for people to get to know. People of the eastern Sudan call it the "gloved cat" because of its white toes, and still tame it from the wild.

People who study cats think that Felis lybica's tame offspring spread all around the world, probably carried on sailing ships. However, in different countries, other wildcats may have bred with the lybica-type cats to create something new. For instance, the European wild cat, *Felis silvestris*, may be in the pussycat family tree. This cat lives in forests all across Europe and western Asia. The European wild cat weighs 4.5 to 11 kg (10 to 24 lbs.) and looks like a particularly big, tough black-striped tabby cat. Dark-striped tabbies are very common in northern Europe. Maybe they got their looks from silvestris. They got their mild manners somewhere else, though. People have had little luck taming European wild cats, even when they start with kittens.

Grow Some Fun for Your Cat

The chemical in catnip that makes cats behave so strangely is called *nepetalactone*. But no one knows *why* it makes cats roll on the floor and generally act foolish.

Things You'll Need:

a package of catnip seeds

a sunny spot in your garden or

a plant pot on a sunny windowsill (choose a room that you can keep your cat out of, or the catnip will be eaten before the plants can mature)

string

1. You can buy catnip seed packets at a garden center, or you can send away for them. (See page 4.)
2. Follow the package instructions for planting the seeds. Catnip isn't a hard plant to grow — it needs some sun and it needs to be watered every few days, but not soaked. It takes about two weeks for the seeds to germinate (start to sprout), and about three months for the plants to mature. It's a *perennial* plant, which means it will grow back again, year after year.
3. If you planted your catnip outside in the spring, it will be ready to harvest in late summer. Pull up a few of the plants. Gather them in bundles and tie them with string. Hang the bundles upside down in a dry, indoor place. (Put them somewhere where eager paws can't pull them down!)
4. When the leaves and flowers are dry and crumbly, you can give them to your cat a pinch at a time. (Store the rest in a plastic bag in the refrigerator or freezer.)
5. You can also use catnip to stuff a cat toy. (See page 62.)

Mau the Sacred Cat

The family was dressed in mourning clothes. They had shaved off their eyebrows as a sign of grief. They wept and wrung their hands as the body of their friend was prepared for burial. Linen mummy wrappings were wound carefully around her body. Her beautiful collar of turquoise stones was placed around her neck for the last time. Her body was gently laid in a carved wooden coffin inlaid with gold and jewels. Then the grieving family carried her to the temple of Bubastis for burial. There they said their last goodbyes to their beloved cat.

In Egypt, 4,000 years ago, cats were loved and respected. They were prized because they kept mice from eating the stored grain. They kept poison snakes from invading people's homes. And their bird-hunting skills were put to use. A painting from an Egyptian tomb shows a large tabby cat being taken along on a family hunting expedition — it has a duck pinned under each paw, and is catching a third one in its mouth! (If you ever go to the British Museum in London, England, you can see this painting for yourself.) Other paintings show cats as well-treated members of the family. In one, a cat is under a chair eating a fish while the family is having a banquet.

If the family cat got sick, it was tended as carefully as a sick child. The cat received the best medical care the family could afford. If the house was on fire, people were supposed to rescue the cat first. The penalty for killing a cat, even by accident, was death. If someone found a dead cat in the street, he would run away, wailing about the terrible thing that had happened. That way, he hoped, no one would think he had killed the cat.

According to one historian of ancient times, Egypt lost a battle because of its love for cats. When the Persian king

Cambyses invaded Egypt in 500 B.C. , he ordered his soldiers to carry live cats in front of them as shields. The Egyptians surrendered, rather than risk killing a cat by fighting back.

The ancient Egyptian word for "cat" was *mau*. This was also the Egyptian word for "seeing" or "light." Because mau sounds so much like "meow," some writers have guessed that mau was the word for cat *first*, and later became the word for "light." Like many later people, the Egyptians were impressed by cats' large eyes and the way they glowed in the dark. Egyptian women used to draw heavy black lines around their eyes. Probably this was to make them look more like the cats they admired.

One of the most important ancient Egyptian gods was Bastet. Her statues show her with the head of a cat and the slender body of a woman. She holds a stringed musical instrument called a *systrum* and often carries a basket of kittens. She was the goddess of the moon, of motherhood and of good health. Her temple, at Bubastis, was considered the most beautiful in Egypt. Sacred cats roamed the gardens of this temple and were cared for by priests.

People carried *amulets* (good luck charms) with pictures of cats and the name of Bastet on them. When a couple got married, they were given a special charm showing a cat with her kittens. The number of kittens was supposed to predict the number of children the couple would have!

While Egypt was strong, its people protected their cats. Anyone caught trying to steal a cat was executed. The Egyptian kingdom finally fell to the Romans in 58 B.C. From then on, wherever the Roman armies marched, they took cats with them. But to the Romans, and to the people in the countries they conquered, cats were mouse-catchers, not gods. For cats, life would never be the same again.

Calling All Cats

Some cats come when they're called—some of the time. Why not try calling to your cat in a foreign language? *Here, Neko, Neko, Neko!* If it doesn't come, you can tell yourself it's because your cat doesn't understand Japanese!

Language	Word for "Cat"
Latin	felis
Arabic	qitt
French	chat
Spanish and Portuguese	gato
Italian	gatto
Greek	gata
Polish	kot
Russian	koshka
German	katze
Ancient Egyptian	mau
Chinese	mao
Indonesian	kutjing
Japanese	neko
Hebrew	chatul
Cree	puje

Lifesaving Cats

What was the matter with Ralph? The little cat kept running up the basement stairs into the house. As soon as he got his owner's attention, Ralph would scamper back to the basement again, yowling as loudly as he could. Finally, the man followed Ralph downstairs. There he heard faint cries for help — and found his daughter trapped in a walk-in freezer. Ralph's fussing had saved her life.

Baby was a deaf cat who had never learned to meow. Just the same, she saved her owner when he had a heart attack. Over and over again, she hurled herself onto the bed where the man's wife was sleeping. At last the woman awoke, in time to get help for her husband.

For over 20 years, the Ralston Purina Company has been honoring heroic cats like Ralph and Baby. (They've also honored many dogs and even one horse.) Animals that have shown great bravery or loyalty can become members of the Purina Animal Hall of Fame. Maybe *you* know of a cat or other animal who recently did something brave to help people. Write and tell the Ralston Purina Company all about it at this address:

> Animal Hall of Fame
> Ralston Purina Canada Inc.
> 2500 Royal Windsor Drive
> Mississauga, Ontario
> L5J 1K8

Write your name and address clearly on your letter so that Ralston Purina can send you a reply.

Bad Times, Good Times

The black cat fled into a twisting, dark street in the oldest part of town. When she came to a rotting wooden gate, she quickly squeezed underneath it. Then she crouched behind the gate, heart pounding, as the man went by. On his back he carried a wriggling sack. Horrible yowls and hisses came from the sack, filling the cat with terror. Tonight she would gather up her kittens and move them out to the fields. From now on, she would stay away from human beings.

For hundreds of years, starting in the tenth century, cats in England, France and other European countries were hunted and killed. These were the darkest times in cat history. Many people thought that cats, especially black ones, were witches in disguise, or messengers of the devil.

If a cat was seen near a house where someone became sick, or near fields where the crops weren't growing well, people were sure the cat was to blame. Hundreds of cats were caught and thrown onto bonfires on holidays. It was dangerous just to own a cat. One woman was hanged for witchcraft because a neighbor saw a cat jump through her window one evening.

Somehow cats survived in Europe until better times came. Probably there were always some people who liked and protected them. In other parts of the world, cats were treated more kindly. In Thailand (which used to be called Siam) and Myanmar (which used to be called Burma), cats held almost as high a position as they had in ancient Egypt. People of the Buddhist religion believed that when very worthy people died, their souls entered the bodies of cats. Sacred cats were fed and cared for in temples.

In Japan, cats were kept indoors as well-loved pets. They were never let outside to hunt. But, in the meantime, mice were gobbling up silkworm cocoons, which the Japanese used to make silk cloth. People tried putting pictures and statues of cats near the silkworms to scare off the mice. This didn't work very well, as you might guess. Finally, in 1602, laws were passed that sent the cats back to work.

By the late 1600s, cats were in favor again in Europe. In England, a famous scientist, Sir Isaac Newton, invented a cat door with a flap. Then his cats could go in and out whenever they pleased. In France, Charles Perrault wrote one of the world's most famous cat stories, *Puss in Boots*. It tells of a clever cat who makes his owner wealthy. Rich and famous Europeans were painted holding their pet cats.

By this time, cats from Europe were being taken to North America. The first cats to arrive were two skilled rat-catchers. French missionaries brought them as a gift for the Huron people. The Hurons had never seen such animals before,

SURPRISING FACTS ABOUT CATS

The Hotel with Something Extra

The rambling old Anderson House hotel in Wabasha, Minnesota has home cooking and cosy, comfortable rooms. It also has ten gentle, friendly cats who are lent to guests for the night. The hotel supplies their food and kitty litter, too. The most popular cat is huge, orange Morris, who looks something like the TV commercial star. Other favorite cats are Sydney the heavyweight Siamese, cheerful black Aloysius, and a striped cat named Tiger. People returning to the hotel for another stay often book their favorite pussycat months in advance. One guest asked especially for cuddly Ginger, explaining that he made a great foot-warmer on cold winter nights!

because there were no tame cats in North America. By the 1700s, settlers all along the east coast of North America were begging captains of sailing ships to bring them some cats. Their stored grain was being eaten by rats and mice.

About a hundred years ago, people began to breed cats and hold cat shows. For these people, it made no difference whether a cat could catch mice or not. What counted was the silkiest coat, the fluffiest tail, the brightest blue eyes, or the daintiest paws. Many other people took cats into their homes as pets. And that's where most of them — the lucky ones — are now. Cats today aren't treated as gods, as they were in ancient times. But they're much better off than their ancestors who were hunted as witches.

Strange Cat Superstitions

Have you ever heard somebody say that it's bad luck if a black cat crosses your path? This idea has been around for hundreds of years, ever since the days when cats were thought to be demons.

In North America and many countries in Europe, some people still believe that black cats are unlucky. In England, though, people think black cats bring *good* luck. The English say that white cats are unlucky, because they're the color of ghosts. In Japan and some other Asian countries, tortoiseshell cats — the ones with black and orange blotches — are considered lucky.

Here are a few other strange cat superstitions:

- In Eastern Europe, people used to think that evil spirits took shelter inside cats' bodies during storms. They believed that angels hurled lightning bolts to drive the spirits out. Whenever there was a storm, people made their cats go outside so that the house wouldn't be hit by lightning.

- In ancient China, people believed they could tell the time of day by looking at a cat's eyes. They said that the cat's pupils became narrower as the morning passed. At noon, the pupils were narrow slits. Then the pupils would slowly open again as the afternoon advanced.

- Indonesian farmers used cats as rainmakers. They would carry a cat around their parched field three times. Then they would dunk the cat in water to show it what they wanted.

- In Russia, people used to put a cat in a cradle before a baby was born. They believed the cat would drive away any evil spirits lurking there.

Ready, Set, Pounce!

Your cat's curiosity and fast paws will make these games fun for both of you.

1. Bubble Burst

Things You'll Need:
bubble blowing mix — buy it at a store or mix up a batch of your own:

1 L (1 qt.) water

15 mL (1 tbsp.) liquid detergent

5 mL (1 tsp.) sugar

45-60 mL (3-4 tbsp.) glycerine (buy at a drugstore)

1. Blow some bubbles toward your cat. Some cats will make a grab for a bubble right away. Others will watch for a while, as the bubbles drift lazily past their noses, changing shape and color.
2. Sooner or later, your cat will bat at a bubble. Of course, the bubble will burst. The cat will likely stare at its wet paw in disbelief — where did that thing go? Most cats will keep trying to scoop a bubble out of the air. They seem to enjoy the challenge, even if they never succeed.

2. Batter Up!

Things You'll Need:
some ping-pong balls or other *very light* balls

1. Put your cat on a table where it can be at eye level with you.
2. Toss a ping-pong ball straight up in front of the cat, about 15 cm (6 ins.) away from the cat's nose. If your cat is in a playful mood, it will probably take a swipe at the ball.
3. Keep tossing the balls up in front of the cat. Most cats love to match their wits and paws against the fast-moving balls. They may miss a few at first, but with practice, their aim will get better and better. Soon your cat will be batting close to 1.000.

P.S. Does your cat use both paws to bat the balls, or does it favor one paw? See "Is There a Southpaw in the House?" on p. 48.

The Long and Short of It

Most of the cats you see in your neighborhood are *mixed-breed* cats. They come in all colors and body shapes. Most are short-haired, but a few have long fur. Usually, their parents were cats who chose their own mates. *Purebred* cats are cats whose mates are carefully chosen for them by people.

A little over 100 years ago, people became interested in mating cats with special features — long fur, or silver-grey coats, or blue eyes — so that their kittens would carry on these features. Breeders began to hold shows in which their cats could compete. They made lists of the features that various cat breeds should have. The prize-winning cats would be the ones who came closest to having all the features on the list. Today, cat associations in Europe and North America recognize around 50 different breeds of cat. Here are just a few of them.

LONG-HAIRS

The first **Persian** cats were brought to Europe, and later North America, from Asia. No one knows exactly where in Asia they first lived, but Persians look like they may have come from a cold place. These cats have long, silky coats with a shorter layer of fluff underneath. They have a showy ruff of fur around their necks. Tufts of fur grow out of their ears and between their toes. Their faces are round and their noses are flat. Persians have stocky bodies with short, solid legs. They are usually quiet, gentle cats who would rather lie in the sun than chase after toys.

Persians come in many beautiful colors. For instance, there are white Persians with blue eyes, blue Persians (actually a blue-grey color) with copper eyes, and Persians with mixed coat colors such as tabbies (striped fur) and calicoes (orange, white and black fur).

The oldest North American cat breed is the **Maine Coon** cat. People used to say that this breed began when a cat mated with a raccoon. This can't happen, of course — cats can only mate with other cats. But when you look at one of these cats, you can see how the story got started. Many of them have brown tabby fur and bushy, ringed tails. Maine coon cats are one of the biggest breeds. Males can weigh more than 7 kg (15 lbs). These sturdy cats have thick, shaggy coats, well suited for cold Maine winters.

Himalayans are one of the newer cat breeds. In spite of their exotic-sounding name, they have nothing to do with Nepal or Tibet. They were first bred in the United States in the 1930s, by crossing Siameses with Persians. They have a Persian's long coat, stocky body and round face, and a Siamese's markings and blue eyes.

SHORT-HAIRS

Siamese cats were brought to the Western world from Thailand (which used to be called Siam) in the 1880s. They are small, lean cats with dainty paws, long tails, and wedge-shaped heads. Their short coats are pale and there are "points" of darker fur on their heads, tails and paws. Siameses are active cats with loud meows that sound to some people like a crying baby. In Siam, these cats were kept in temples and at the royal palace. The penalty for taking one of these cats out of the country was death. (Daring thieves made off with them, anyway, just as they did in ancient Egypt.)

A lot of the early Siamese cats had bent tails and crossed eyes. There is a story that their eyes became crossed from staring so hard at the temple vases they were guarding. Another story tells of a royal princess who put her rings on her cat's tail while she went swimming. The rings slipped off and were lost, so the next time she tied a knot in the

Persian cats have long, silky coats.

cat's tail to keep her rings in place. From then on, Siamese cats had kinked tails. (Of course, heredity does not really work this way.)

Abyssinians are a very old breed. Their admirers like to believe they are descended from the sacred cats of ancient Egypt. With their long legs and big, pointed ears, they certainly look like the cats in Egyptian wall paintings and sculptures. Abyssinians have short, thick *agouti* coats. "Agouti" means that each coat hair has a yellowish middle section and a dark brown tip. Many wild mammals have fur like this, because the pattern makes them hard to see as they crouch in the woods. Abyssinians are the only domestic cats with such a coat.

Manx cats can have many different coat colors, but they all have one thing in common — they have no tails. The breed takes its name from the Isle of Man, where there were many tailless cats. There's an old story that the Manx cat was the last animal to climb aboard Noah's ark. It lost its tail when Noah accidentally slammed the door too soon. Now we know that there is a *gene* that causes these cats to be born without tails. (What's a gene? It's an instruction inside the body cells of living things that tells them how to grow. Cats — and human beings — inherit their genes from their parents.) Some people think Manx cats should not be bred, because their "no tail" gene sometimes causes spine problems that keep these cats from walking properly.

In a Class By Themselves

Rex cats are thin, big-eared cats with short, curly fur that looks a lot like poodle fur. Even their whiskers have a frizzled look! The first Rex kitten was born in Cornwall, England in 1950. All its brothers and sisters had straight fur. The owner went to some cat breeders and asked them how to breed more cats like this unusual kitten, and this was the beginning of the Cornish Rex breed.

The **Sphynx** is a cat with almost no hair at all. Like the Rex, the breed began with a single kitten in a litter with ordinary fur. This kitten was born in Ontario in 1966. Some breeders think frizzy cats and bald cats should not be bred on purpose. They say these animals are too far away from what cats should look like. What do you think?

Can Your Cat Hear You?

How can you tell whether your cat is living in a silent world?

1. Look at your cat's coat and eye color

White cats with yellow or green eyes can usually hear, but about half of white *blue-eyed* cats are deaf. Cats of other colors can be deaf from birth, too, but it's unusual. Only about one in a hundred nonwhite cats is born with no hearing.

2. Has your cat had a head injury or a bad ear infection?

Some cats have hearing problems after their heads are injured in a car accident or fall. An ear infection can also cause a cat to lose its hearing. (Cats with ear infections often shake their heads or paw at their ears.)

3. Is your cat more than 10 years old?

Older cats, like older people, sometimes don't hear as well as they once did.

4. How does your cat behave?

Cats who are born deaf may never learn to meow. Cats who hear little or nothing won't come running when you use the can opener. They may sleep more. But other cats, quiet cats or lazy cats, may act this way too. How can you test your cat's hearing?

(a) Wait until your cat is lying down and relaxed. Stand behind the cat so that it can't see you. Clap your hands loudly and call its name. If the cat is startled, it can hear you.

(b) If the cat doesn't move a muscle, try this. Stamp your feet hard on the floor. Even deaf cats will probably leap up. Why? Your stamping causes a vibration (shaking) that the cat can feel.

(c) If your cat reacts only to stamping, there's a good chance it's deaf. Take your cat to a veterinarian to have its ears checked. The vet may be able to tell you what is causing your cat's hearing problem.

Remember, pets who can't hear can still have very happy lives. Just show them some extra kindness. Make sure your cat knows that it's mealtime, even if it can't hear the can opener. Try to approach your cat from the front, so it won't be startled when you suddenly pet it or pick it up. Your cat should probably stay inside. Outside, it would be in more danger than other cats because it can't hear cars coming.

A Family in Danger

Have you ever seen a lion at the zoo, licking one of its huge paws and then washing its face? "Awww, isn't that sweet?" exclaim the onlookers. "Just like a great big pussycat!" Have you ever seen a house cat getting ready to pounce on a catnip toy? It slinks forward on its belly; it stops, haunches twitching, and then it springs! It looks just like a lion leaping on its prey in a wildlife TV program.

All over the world, large or small, wild or tame, members of the cat family have a lot in common. All of them have rounded heads with big eyes, stiff fans of whiskers, and sharp fangs. All of them are agile, light-footed hunters, built for sprinting, jumping and climbing.

Zoologists (scientists who study animals) have set up a system for classifying the different kinds of cats. All the names in this system are in Latin. Why Latin? Scientists first worked at classifying animals about 200 years ago. At that time, Latin was the language educated people from different countries used to speak to each other.

Today, it's still useful to have a system everyone can agree on. For instance, there's a big North American cat that some people call a mountain lion. Did you know that cougar is just another name for the same animal? In South America it's called a puma. You can see how confusing this can get. So zoologists,no matter where in the world they live, call this cat by its Latin name, *Felis concolor*.

The Latin name of the whole cat family is *Felidae*. There are 37 different species of cats in the family. They're divided into three groups. The first group, *Panthera*, has six big cats: lions, tigers, leopards, snow leopards, clouded leopards, and jaguars. Although people call the African lion the King of the Beasts, the Asian tiger is bigger. Tigers can weigh more than 270 kg (600 lbs.), while lions weigh about 180 kg (400 lbs.).

Cheetahs are the fastest land animals on earth.

24

Leopards, too, are cats of Africa and Asia. The jaguar is the only Panthera cat found in North and South America. All these cats have a special kind of voice box for thunderous roars.

The second group, *Acinonyx*, has only one cat in it: the cheetah (see page 27 for more about this cat). The third group, *Felis*, is the biggest, with 29 species of cats. Your pet cat, known as *Felis catus*, is in this group. *Felis* cats are found all over the world. Most weigh 14 kg (30 lbs.) or less. The smallest is the Rusty Spotted Cat (*Felis rubiginosa*) of India and Sri Lanka, which only weighs about 1.3 kg (3 lbs.). The one *Felis* heavyweight is the mountain lion (*Felis concolor*) which can weigh up to 90 kg (200 lbs.). *Felis* cats can growl, meow, purr and hiss, but they can't roar.

The sad thing about the proud family of *Felidae* is that most of them are on the World Wildlife Fund's endangered list. Unless people begin to protect them better, there won't be any wildcats left outside of zoos. The big cats have always been targets of hunters who wanted to prove how brave they were by killing them. It may have taken bravery to kill a big cat with a spear, but even the fiercest tiger has no chance against a modern high-powered rifle. Some cats, including ocelots and leopards, have been hunted for their beautiful coats. Many countries no longer allow the sale of such furs, and many people refuse to wear them. But for some cat species, these measures may have come too late.

Today, cats share a terrible problem with all the other large meat-eating animals. They need big territories where they can hunt their prey. As jungles and forests all over the world are being cut down to make more pasture or farmland, these animals are losing their homes. We are just beginning to realize that human beings also need forests to survive. The Amazon rainforests are called the "lungs of the earth" because they help to keep our air clean. If we save forests where cats can roam free, we'll also be saving ourselves.

Odd Cat Out

Cheetahs are such unusual cats that people who study the cat family put them in a group all their own — *Acinonyx*. The cheetah is the only cat that can't retract (pull in) its claws all the way. When it runs, its claws dig into the ground to keep it from slipping. In fact, everything about the cheetah is built for speed. It has long legs, a deep chest with powerful lungs, and a slim, streamlined body.

Over short distances, the cheetah is the fastest land animal on earth. From a standing start, it can reach its top speed of over 100 km/h (over 60 mph) in just three seconds. Its prey are fleet-footed antelopes, who are not quite as fast as cheetahs. Still, the cheetah doesn't always win — antelopes can change direction faster and run longer distances.

Today, like many other wildcats, cheetahs are losing their struggle to survive. Once they were found in the dry open plains of Africa, Arabia, Iran and India. But the land where the antelope used to graze is being taken over by farms, leaving the cheetahs without food. Some people hunt cheetahs illegally, for sport or for their fur. Now there are only a few hundred cheetahs left in the wild in Asia and in African game parks.

The Cheetah (Acinonyx jubatus)
Home: Africa, southern Asia
Weight: 38 to 64 kg (85 to 140 lbs.)
Food: small antelope and deer
Hunts in the daytime

Snowshoe Cats

When you think of wildcats, do you picture them lurking in steamy jungles or prowling on sunbaked plains? Did you know that Canada has its own wildcat — the lynx — who is right at home in the snowy northern woods? The lynx grows a thick, soft coat to keep it warm in winter. When it spreads its toes apart, its feet turn into wide, flat "snowshoes." These big furry feet let the lynx run on snow without breaking through.

The lynx's main prey is the snowshoe hare. When there are lots of hares, there is plentiful food for the lynxes, and many lynx babies are born. As the babies grow up, they eat more and more hares. After a few years, there aren't enough hares to feed them. Then the lynxes begin to starve and their numbers go down. With fewer lynxes to eat them, the hare population begins to grow again. Once more there are lots of hares for lynxes to eat, and the whole cycle — which lasts about ten years — starts again.

Lynx canadensis
Home: forested areas of Canada and the northeastern and northcentral United States
Weight: 8 to 11 kg (18 to 25 lbs.)
Food: snowshoe hares (more than three-quarters of a lynx's diet); also birds, mice, squirrels
Hunts at night

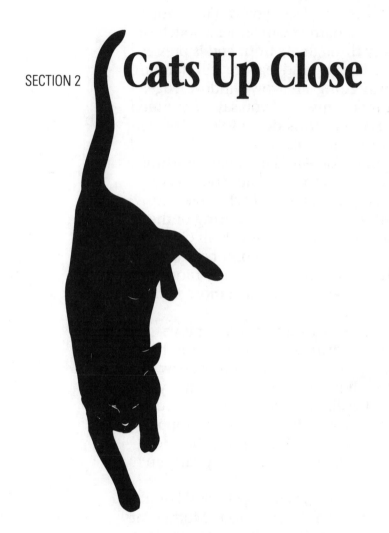

Cats Up Close

Four-Footed Gymnasts

If you try to follow your cat around the house or neighborhood, you'll soon find there are places you can't go. Your cat can squeeze through the narrow gap under a couch or fence. When it is halfway through, its front end is pressed flat against the ground while its hind legs are still standing. Later, the cat picks its way along a narrow window ledge. "Well, of course I can't follow my cat," you say. "I'm much bigger!" But even if you could shrink down to cat-size, your human body couldn't move like a cat's.

All mammals, including people and cats, have a string of bones called *vertebrae* in their backs. These bones are separated by cushiony pads called *discs*. Each bone and disc can only move a little bit, but a whole string of them can move a lot. (The plastic "pop-it" beads small children play with work like this, too. One bead won't bend or twist, but a string of them will.) A cat has many more bones in its spine than you do, so it is much more *flexible* (able to bend).

A cat's legs are jointed in a way that lets them move much more freely than your arms and legs. A cat can hurry along a 5 cm (2 inch) ledge, putting its right front paw down in a straight line with its left front paw. Even if you were as small as a cat and walking on all fours, you couldn't put your hands and feet in a straight line without toppling over. Human gymnasts use a 9 cm (4 inch) wide balance beam, and they still have to practice before they can run along it without falling.

A cat's loose-fitting skin also helps it to twist and bend freely. The skin is loosest around the cat's neck. Mother cats use this loose skin to carry their kittens. If an enemy tries to bite the cat's neck, the loose skin gives the cat a good chance of pulling away.

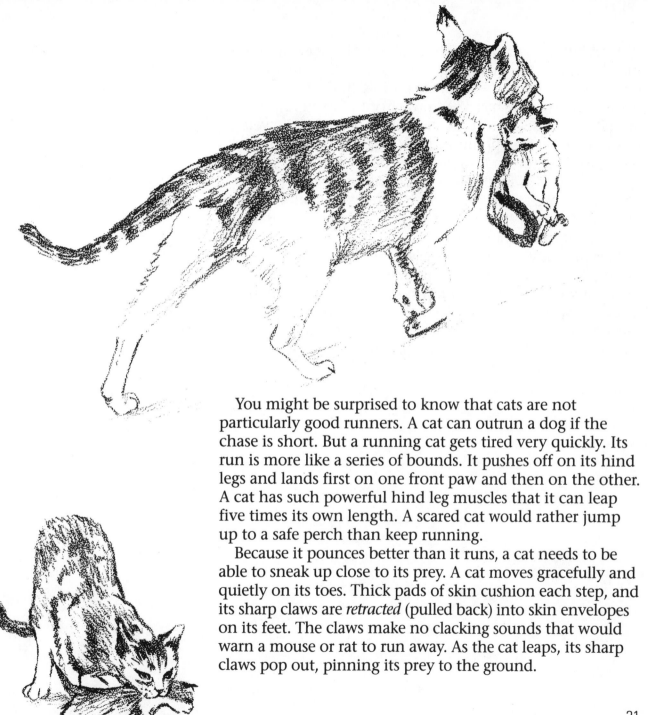

You might be surprised to know that cats are not particularly good runners. A cat can outrun a dog if the chase is short. But a running cat gets tired very quickly. Its run is more like a series of bounds. It pushes off on its hind legs and lands first on one front paw and then on the other. A cat has such powerful hind leg muscles that it can leap five times its own length. A scared cat would rather jump up to a safe perch than keep running.

Because it pounces better than it runs, a cat needs to be able to sneak up close to its prey. A cat moves gracefully and quietly on its toes. Thick pads of skin cushion each step, and its sharp claws are *retracted* (pulled back) into skin envelopes on its feet. The claws make no clacking sounds that would warn a mouse or rat to run away. As the cat leaps, its sharp claws pop out, pinning its prey to the ground.

A cat kills its prey with a sharp bite to the neck. It uses its piercing fangs, the matching pair of long, sharp teeth on each side of its mouth. An adult cat has 30 teeth in all. (An adult human being has 32.) In the front of its mouth there are 12 tiny chisel-shaped teeth (six uppers and six lowers). These are used for ripping and scraping. It also has 14 back teeth (four on top and three on the bottom on each side). A cat can't chew its food into a mush the way we can. Instead, its back teeth work together like the blades of scissors. They cut the food into bite-sized pieces so that the cat can gulp them down.

To get at those last little morsels of meat clinging to the bones, the cat uses its raspy tongue. If you've ever been licked by a friendly cat, you know just how rough a cat's tongue is. That's because the center of a cat's tongue is covered with little hooks. These hooks are also handy for combing through the cat's coat when it is giving itself a wash.

PAWS-itively Exhausting!

Cats is a musical show in which 34 very fit, very talented performers pretend to be cats. *Cats* has been staged all over the world, including several cities in Canada. To help them look like cats, the performers wear stretchy leotards that are striped, spotted, or furry. They also paint their faces like cats — the makeup takes almost two hours to put on. But that's the easy part. The hard part is moving like cats for almost three hours onstage. Human bodies just aren't made to do the things cats can do so easily.

During a two-year run of *Cats* in Toronto, the cast members sucked on 84,000 lozenges to soothe throats worn out by singing, yowling, and hissing. The woman who played Grisabella, the sad cat who sings "Memories," bruised her vocal cords so badly that she couldn't sing for several months afterwards. The performers always had sore muscles — and sometimes sprains and broken bones — from leaping and stretching. Understudies were always standing by to take over the part of anyone who was injured. In fact, out of 500 performances, there were only 30 with no understudies replacing injured performers!

❖ *Try it Yourself*

Str-r-r-e-e-tch Like a Cat

Have you ever watched a cat waking up from a nap? It stretches out its front legs, and then its hind legs. When *you* stretch like a cat, you'll feel your body loosen up and relax.

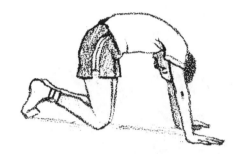

Things You'll Need:
an exercise mat or a soft rug

What to Do:
1. Get down on your hands and knees. Hold your back straight. (It may help to imagine that your back is a table.) Breathe in through your nose and out through your mouth.
2. Now *slowly* raise your back until it's high and rounded. At the same time, curl your head under until you're looking at your knees. Hold this position while you count to five.

3. Flatten your back again. Slowly *str-r-e-e-tch* your right leg out behind you while you raise your head. Count to five. Put your right knee back on the floor.
4. Arch your back and tuck your head under, as you did before. Count to five.
5. Flatten your back again. Slowly *str-r-e-e-tch* your left leg out behind you while you raise your head. Count to five. Then put your left knee back on the floor.

Good Vibrations — and Other Cat Senses

People often say that cats can see in the dark. This isn't quite true. Cats can see better than we do in dim light, but they can't see when there's no light at all. Cats do have something extra to help them find their way at night — *vibrissae*. Vibrissae is the Latin name for whiskers.

Whiskers are special stiff hairs that are more than twice as thick as the cat's other hair. There are about 12 on each side of its nose, a sprinkling on its chin and over each eye, and a few on the back of each front leg. Whiskers are very sensitive to anything they touch. A cat can use its whiskers to check the size of an opening before it tries to go through. It can brush them along the floor to find crumbs of food. Whiskers can also detect air currents. Any solid thing makes little changes in the direction air is moving. Warned by its whiskers that something is near, a cat can avoid the object without seeing or touching it.

Cats can also detect movements of another kind. Did you know that sounds are made by something that is vibrating (shaking back and forth very fast)? These vibrations make the air around the thing vibrate, too. When the vibrations reach an ear — yours or your cat's — the ears hear a sound.

The faster a thing vibrates, the higher the sound it makes. We use Herz (Hz) to measure how fast a sound wave vibrates. Your ears can hear sounds from about 30 Hz (a very deep rumble) to about 20,000 Hz (a very high squeak). Cats can hear the same deep sounds you can, but they can also hear much higher sounds, up to about 65,000 Hz. This is even higher than dogs can hear. Why does a cat need to hear such high-pitched sounds? Perhaps you can guess the answer — mice squeak at about 65,000 Hz.

Cats can also hear softer sounds than we can, because their large, pointed ears are much better at gathering sounds than ours are. Cats have 30 muscles in their ears, so that they can turn them toward a sound. Our ears have only about six muscles, and most of us don't know how to wiggle them, anyway.

Cats are famous for being able to land on their feet. Would you be surprised to know that this has something to do with their ears? Deep inside a cat's ears (and human ears, too) are organs that help it balance and tell it when it is right side up. When a cat begins to fall upside down, it uses these balance organs to turn its head right way up first. Then it uses its powerful muscles and flexible spine to turn the top half of its body. Finally it turns the back half of its body, stretches out its legs, and lands on all four feet. Still, cats don't always land safely. Many have been injured or even killed in falls. Certainly, you should never try dropping one to see if it can right itself.

Cats have a very keen sense of smell. The special area inside their noses that picks up smells is twice as big as the one in your nose. Cats use their sensitive noses to decide whether their food is good to eat. Smells are also an important way cats send messages to each other. Cats, especially male cats, make "scent maps" of their neighborhoods . They rub against trees and other things to mark them with their own special smell. (Sometimes male cats spray their urine on things, too.) Cats also sniff carefully to see what other animals have been there. When a cat smells its own old scent marks, it knows it is safe inside its own territory. Outside its territory, it will probably run away if another cat challenges it. Inside its territory, it will probably chase the other cat away.

Do you find it discouraging to read about all the ways your cat's senses work better than yours? Well, cheer up, your sense of taste is at least as good as your cat's, and maybe better. Cats' bodies are designed for a steady diet of meat. They don't need to be able to taste the range of things people can taste. Like other mammals, including human beings, cats have taste buds for sweet, salty, bitter, and sour things. But cats don't have very many taste buds that can taste sugar. This is probably just as well, because too much sugar upsets cats' stomachs. On the other hand, cats are very sensitive to the taste of water. Pet owners are sometimes shocked when their cats drink from outdoor puddles instead of from their water dishes. It may be that the cats hate the taste of the chemicals added to tap water to kill germs.

Project Tiger

Tigers — the largest cats in the world — once ranged all over Asia. Sixty years ago, there were 40,000 tigers in India alone. Now there are only 7500 wild tigers left in the whole world (and about 1500 more in zoos). In 1970, the World Wildlife Fund started Project Tiger to save the Indian tiger. At that time India had only 1500 tigers left. The Indian government set aside 15 forest reserves where tigers were protected. Now their numbers have started to creep up again, and are at about 4,000.

It was hard for India, which is poor and crowded with people, to set aside reserves. However, the government realized that the whole environment — water, plants, the air — becomes healthier for people as well as animals in areas where there are reserves. There are still problems, though. The reserves are small. The tigers tend to wander off them because they need large hunting territories. They especially like to lurk in the tall plants of sugar cane plantations, waiting for prey. Unfortunately, that prey is sometimes human. Tigers are one of the few cat species that will kill and eat people. (Only about one tiger in a hundred is a "man-eater." Often that tiger is too old or sick to catch stronger, faster prey.) As the number of people needing farmland grows, and the number of tigers increases, will people still protect the tiger?

Eye Spy

People have always been fascinated by cats' eyes. They come in vivid shades of blue, hazel, green, yellow, and orange. They're also very large. Human eyeballs are about 24 mm (1 inch) across. Even though cats' faces are much smaller than people's, their eyeballs are almost as big — about 22 mm (7/8 inch) across.

Cats' eyes are much more changeable than ours. In bright sunlight, our pupils (the black circles in the center of our eyes) become smaller, but cats' pupils close down to a hairline. Even stranger is the way cats' eyes glow when a light shines on them at night. This spooky "nightshine" probably helped to convince people in the Middle Ages that cats were evil.

For all their strangeness, cats' eyes work a lot like yours. Eyes work by taking in light that reflects off objects. Bright things reflect a lot of light; dark things reflect only a little light. Light enters your eye (and your cat's eye) through the *cornea*. This is the transparent ("see-through") bulge on the front of the eye. Behind the cornea is the *iris*, the colored part of the eye. The *pupil*, the opening that lets light into the eye, is in the center of the iris. It looks black because the eye is dark inside.

A ring of muscles in your iris controls how much light gets into your eye. If there's lots of light, the muscles squeeze to make the pupil smaller. If it's dark, the muscles relax to let the pupils get bigger and let in more light. Cats' pupils can open up wider than yours in dim light, to let in every last bit of light. In bright light, cats' iris muscles can close the pupil down to a slit.

40

Just inside the pupil is a clear *lens*. It's attached to muscles that can pull it so that it changes shape. The lens bends the light coming into the eye. This makes the rays of light *focus* (form a clear image) on the back of the eye. Cats' lens muscles are weaker than yours, and they don't focus as well. You see the fine details of things better than they do. However, they have a wider view of things than you have because their lenses are bigger. Cats are great at spotting movement, especially to the side. This must come in handy when they are hunting field mice in the grass.

At the back of the eye, on the inside, is the *retina*. Your retina is made up of over a million special cells that are sensitive to light. These cells are joined to nerves that send sight messages to your brain. There are two main kinds of retina cells. They are named *rods* and *cones* because of their shapes.

Cones let you see in color. Some cones see only red light, some see only blue light, and some see only green light. These cones also work together. For instance, if both blue and green cones are at work, you can see a bluish-green color called *cyan*. Cones work well in bright light. In dim light, you use your rod cells. Rods can only see in black, white and grey. In your room at night, have you noticed that you can see the shapes of things but not their colors?

Cats have cones and rods, too. But they have fewer bright-light cones and more dim-light rods. People who study cats' eyes believe that cats have cones only for blue and green, not for red. If you could see through your cat's eyes in the daytime, you might find the view disappointing. Your favorite red jacket would look dirty grey. You wouldn't be able to tell traffic lights apart.

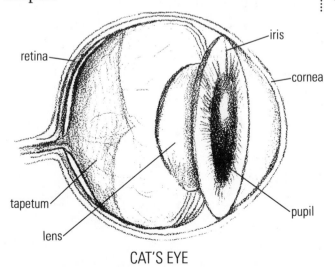

CAT'S EYE

retina

iris

cornea

tapetum

lens

pupil

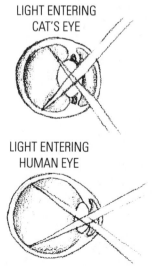

LIGHT ENTERING CAT'S EYE

LIGHT ENTERING HUMAN EYE

But suppose you could see through your cat's eyes at night. What an amazing difference! Out in the woods, far from city lights, you'd be able to see small night animals scurrying around. Cats' retinas have a lot more rods than your eyes do. Behind the retina is an extra layer called the *tapetum*. The tapetum acts like a mirror. When light comes into a cat's eye, the tapetum bounces some of it back through the retina. This means that a cat's retina has two chances to use every last little bit of light. (The tapetum also gives cats their spooky nightshine.) A cat's eyes are much better in dim light than yours. In fact, cats need only one-sixth of the light people need to see things.

Although human eyes see better in the daytime, and cats' eyes do better at night, there's one important way they are alike. Both you and your cat have "hunters' eyes." This means that your eyes are on the front of your head and work together. When you look at something, two images (a little different from each other) are sent to your brain. Your brain puts the images together into one 3-D picture.

With two eyes working together, you can judge how thick something is and how far away it is. Try bringing two fingers together in front of your face with one eye closed. It's very hard to tell when they're lined up! Open both eyes, and you can do it easily.

Cats' eyes work together too. A cat needs to know exactly where its prey is before it pounces. Animals that eat plants don't need to judge distance so well, because plants don't run away. What animals like mice and deer need to know is whether a meat-eater is creeping up on them. Their eyes are farther back on the sides of their heads. Each eye sees something different, so the eyes can't work together to form a 3-D picture. But these animals don't need to see details to survive. If they sense the slightest movement, they flee.

❖ *Try it Yourself*

Night Eyes

Take a look at the mysterious inside of your cat's eyes —
and your own eyes, too.

1. Nightshine

Things You'll Need:
a pen flashlight

a dark room

1. Take your cat and your flashlight into a dark room.
2. Stand about a metre (3 feet) away from your cat. Shine
   the flashlight into its eyes for a couple of seconds. When
   you get the angle just right, the cat's eyes will give off a
   strange green or yellow glow. (A blue-eyed cat's eyes may
   glow red.)

What's Happening?
The light is bouncing off a layer of special cells at the back
of the cat's eyes. They act a lot like bicycle reflectors. Many
animals who hunt at night have this layer in their eyes to
help them see in dim light.

Your eyes will never glow like this, because you don't
have this layer of cells. Find out for yourself what you can
see when you shine a flashlight in your eyes.

2. Mysterious Trees

Things You'll Need:
a pen flashlight

a dark room with a blank, light-colored wall

1. Take your flashlight into a darkened room. Stand facing a blank wall.
2. Close one eye and cover it with your hand.
3. Stare at the wall with your other eye.
4. Hold the flashlight about 30 cm (12 ins.) from your face. Shine the light at the outer edge of your eye. Be careful not to look straight at the flashlight, or you'll be too dazzled to see anything.
5. After a minute or so, you'll see a strange shape on the wall that looks like the branches of a leafless tree. Do you know what it really is? It's an image of all the blood vessels at the back of your own eye!

3. Now You See It!

No matter what you do, you'll never see as well as your cat at night. But there's a little trick to help you see better.

Suppose you're peering into the darkness. Is that a raccoon at the back of the yard, or just a shadow? Instead of looking right at the dark shape, look *just a little* to the side of it. You'll probably see it more clearly. Why? If the light is dim, you're using your rods, not your cones, to see. (Read all about rods and cones on page 41.) There are more rods at the sides of your retina than in the center. If you look to the side, you'll focus the light where your eye can see it best.

Mother Cats and Kittens

Newborn kittens give few signs of the graceful cats they will become. Their legs aren't strong enough to hold them up, but they can crawl for short distances. Kittens are born with their eyes sealed shut and their ears folded flat against their heads. Although they can't see and probably can't hear very well either, they have a keen sense of smell.

Soon after they are born, they nose their way to their mother's nipples and begin to drink her milk. At first, there is a shoving match as the kittens find their places. But the mother cat has eight nipples on her underside, arranged in two rows. Since the average litter has only four kittens, there is enough food for everyone. Soon the kittens recognize their own smell on the nipple they chose, and that becomes their nipple from then on.

A mother cat hardly ever leaves her kittens for the first three weeks of their lives. The kittens spend most of their waking time drinking milk. They may even fall asleep with the nipple in their mouths. If the mother leaves to get a quick meal of her own, her kittens will soon call her back with their loud, shrill cries.

CAT FACTS

Do you know why some cats should *not* drink milk? Do you know how to tell whether a cat toy is safe for your pet? Do you know how to keep a cat from scratching the furniture? The Toronto Humane Society has a 26-page booklet that answers these cat-care questions, and many more. It's packed with advice about how to take care of your new pet and make sure it becomes a happy, healthy member of your family.

Write to:

Toronto Humane Society
11 River Street
Toronto, Ontario
M5A 4C2

Ask for: *Handbook of Cat Care*

Cost: $1.50

Don't forget: Print your own address clearly on your letter, so that they'll know where to send your booklet.

Day by day, the kittens grow bigger and stronger. They double their birth weight in their first week of life. By the end of the second week, their eyes are open and they have their first teeth. In the third week, the kittens begin to scramble in and out of their nest box. When their mother leaves them, they may try to toddle after her. If the mother thinks one of her kittens is straying too far, she will use her teeth to pick it up gently by the scruff of the neck. Then she will carry it back to the nest box.

At around four weeks, the kittens begin to play. They're fun to watch as they make sudden dashes and awkward pounces. They wrestle with each other, holding each other with their front paws. The kitten underneath kicks up furiously with its hind feet. It looks very rough, but no one gets hurt. Although the kittens are having fun, they're also learning how to sneak up on prey and how to defend themselves.

A mother cat who is a hunter will bring home dead prey for the kittens to bat around with their paws. Later, she may even bring home live prey and show the kittens how to kill it. A house-pet mother who has never hunted mice still has a lot to teach her kittens. She takes them to the litter box and shows them how to dig a hole, go in it, and then cover the spot by kicking litter over it. She takes them to her food dish and lets them eat beside her. (And then she washes their faces with her tongue!) She growls and cuffs the kittens with her paw to warn them away from anything she thinks is dangerous. It might be a busy street, a large dog, or even a loud vacuum cleaner.

Little by little, the mother cat lets her kittens make their own way in the world. Instead of staying with them all the time, she sits up on a mantel or windowsill where she can watch them play. As long as they don't look like they're in danger, she leaves them to discover things for themselves. By eight or nine weeks of age, the kittens are ready to start a new life in a new home as somebody's playful pet.

Is There a Southpaw in the House?

Are you left-handed? Only about one in ten human beings is a leftie. Among animals, though, being left-pawed (or hoofed, or flippered) is much more common. Does your cat lead with its left or its right? Try this test to find out.

Things You'll Need:
the cardboard tube from a roll of paper towels

sticky tape

your pet's favorite catfood treats, in small pieces

pencil and paper

1. Tape the cardboard tube to the floor.
2. Most cats will come over and investigate anything new in their homes. Let your pet have a good look at the tube.
3. Put a cat treat in front of the tube's opening. Let your pet find it and eat it.
4. Now put a cat treat just inside the opening of the tube. The cat will have to use its paw to scoop the food out of the tube. Watch to see which paw it uses. Make a note of it.
5. Try the test 10 times, keeping track of which paw your cat uses to get its food. (You may not be able to do all 10 tests at the same time. If your cat gets bored and walks away, wait awhile before finishing the test.)
6. Did your cat use one paw much more than the other? This tells you whether your cat is right or left-pawed. Some cats use both paws equally well. They're called *ambidextrous*. Do you know any ambidextrous people?

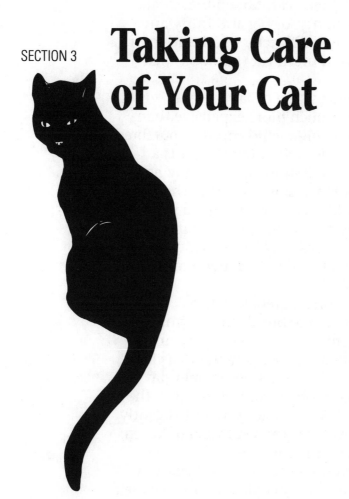

Taking Care of Your Cat

The Right Fluff

Where will you find the right kitten for you? Will it be a purebred kitten or a mixed-breed one? Nearly always, people will choose a mixed-breed cat. Mixed-breed cats can be small and lean and dainty, or big and fluffy and roly-poly. They can be striped or blotchy or all one color. Most people can find a mixed-breed cat that looks just right to them.

What if you have your heart set on a Siamese or a Persian? Purebred kittens are much more expensive than mixed-breed kittens. Often, families who choose a purebred cat plan to enter it in cat shows. If your family wants a purebred house pet rather than a show cat, you may be able to buy one for less money than a show cat costs. The kitten may have "faults" that would keep it from being a prize-winner. For instance, it may have a few stripes in its coat that shouldn't be there, or its ears may be the wrong shape. The cat will still look beautiful to you, and it will make just as good a pet.

If your family has decided on a purebred cat, you will probably buy it from a person who breeds cats or from a pet store. When you buy a cat from a cat breeder, you can see for yourself whether the kittens are being raised in a clean place with good food and kind care. Kittens should stay with their mothers and their brothers and sisters until they are at least eight weeks old. They should be handled gently by people, too, so that the kittens get used to them. Kittens like this will likely be healthy and friendly.

If you want a mixed-breed house pet, you can probably get one cheaply or even free. Many people do not have their female cats operated on to keep them from having kittens. So, every year or so, they eagerly look for someone to take the latest arrivals. If you get your kitten from relatives,

friends, or neighbors, you can tell whether the owners are giving their cats good care. You can also watch the mother and kittens together and see whether the mother is a healthy, good-natured pet. (Bad-tempered, nervous mothers will often have kittens with the same faults.)

Animal shelters, especially those in big cities, are full of cats and kittens who need homes. The shelters keep these animals for as long as they can, but if they do not find homes for them, they are painlessly killed. So if you choose a kitten at an animal shelter, you may be saving a life. (Take your parents with you when you go to the animal shelter. Most shelters will only let adults adopt a pet.)

How can you tell whether a kitten is healthy? Its eyes and nose shouldn't be runny. Its tummy should be firm but not bloated (this means hard and bulging). A bloated tummy can be a sign that the kitten has worms. The kitten should have a shiny, healthy coat. Check its bottom — a wet or stained bottom might mean the kitten has diarrhea. Kind-hearted people often want to take the *runt* of a litter — the kitten that is smaller and weaker than its brothers and sisters. It's not a good idea. This kitten may well have serious health problems.

How can you tell if a kitten is good-natured? If you have a choice of several kittens, take the one that is curious and playful, rather than the shy, timid one. Hold the kitten gently, with one hand under its hind feet, and stroke its fur. In a few minutes it will probably start to purr. You've got yourself a kitten!

SOMETHING TO SEND FOR

BABY CARE

Looking after a baby is a big responsibility. Baby cats, like baby human beings, are small, big-eyed, and cute — and a great deal of work. Kittens need special food, they need to be kept safe, and they need loving, gentle care.

Pets Magazine has a 60-page guide that tells you all about caring for your new kitten or puppy. It's written for adults, but you and your family can read it together.

Write to:
Moorshead Publications
1300 Don Mills Road
North York, Ontario
M3B 3M8

Ask for: Care Guide for Puppies and Kittens

Cost: $2.00

Don't forget: Print your own address clearly on your letter, so they'll know where to send your guide.

Koko's Kittens

It would be hard to pick the world's most unusual pet. People give loving care to tarantulas, boa constrictors, and many other uncuddly creatures. But what about the world's most unusual pet *owner*? That's easy. Her name is Koko, and she's a 100 kg (230 lb.) gorilla.

Of course, Koko is a very special gorilla. She has been taught to speak to people in sign language. She knows over 500 signs and even makes up her own names for things. (She calls people she doesn't like "dirty bad toilets"!) Koko has always loved storybooks about cats. One day she told her trainer, Dr. Francine Patterson, that she would like to have a pet cat of her own. Dr. Patterson gave her a fluffy grey kitten with no tail.

Koko called the kitten All-Ball. She loved her pet and treated her very kindly, cuddling her gently and kissing her. Koko even learned to make purring sounds like All-Ball. When All-Ball was killed by a car, Koko was grief-stricken. These days, though, Koko is a happy pet-owner again, taking care of a grey cat she calls Smoke.

The Stray Cat Blues

Sometimes a kitten — or a cat — chooses *you*. It follows you home or turns up at your back door, meowing and demanding attention. What happens next depends on your family, not just on you. Some families take in strays; some don't. If yours doesn't, you should at least phone the humane society to let them know there's a homeless animal wandering around your place. They will come and pick it up.

For animal-loving families, it's a great feeling to "save" a stray. But use your head as well as your heart. If the animal at your door is clean and well-fed , it hasn't been lost for long. In fact, it may just be a friendly neighborhood cat who likes to visit. Don't be too quick to take the cat in and

make it yours. If the cat has been hanging around for several days or if it's cold outside, you may have to bring it in. Put up some signs in your neighborhood saying you've found a cat. Ask the other kids if they know of anyone who's lost a cat. Wouldn't you like someone to make this effort if *your* cat were lost?

You may find a stray that's in terrible shape. If its ribs are sticking out and its fur is matted, there's no doubt it's homeless. It's safer if you *don't* handle a stray cat that is injured or behaving strangely. It may claw you even though you're trying to help. There's a chance it may have rabies, a serious disease that people can catch from animals. Ask an adult for help in dealing with the animal.

Suppose the stray is friendly and alert, but seems hungry, cold and dirty. If you take it in and feed it, keep it in one small part of your house at first, away from other pets. If you're thinking of keeping the stray, it *must* go to a veterinarian for medical care right away. It may have fleas, worms or earmites. It may have injuries that are hidden by its fur. It may be sick. The veterinarian can give you advice about how to bring the kitten back to health. Sometimes strays are too sick to save, but at least you'll know you've done your best. More often, with time, your little waif will turn into a healthy, playful pet. Good luck!

A Real-Life Feline Fairy Tale

There was once a big orange tomcat in a cage at the animal shelter. He sat there day after day, but no one would adopt him. People wanted the fluffy little kittens, not the full-grown cat with the scowling face. (He wasn't really bad-tempered, but no one took the time to find that out.) Then, when his time had almost run out, he was adopted by an animal trainer named Bob Martwick. Martwick made the unwanted tom into the most famous cat in North America — Morris.

Morris starred in TV commercials as the finicky eater who wouldn't touch anything but his favorite brand of cat food. He worked only 20 days a year and lived in luxury the rest of the time. When Morris died of old age in 1978 (no one knew exactly how old he was, of course) he wasn't easy to replace. Many people thought they had orange cats who looked just like Morris, but looks weren't enough. A TV cat has to be calm and patient. It must be willing to work under hot lights, repeating a little bit of action over and over until it's just right. The original Morris would even put up with having water thrown on him!

Finally, after a two-and-a-half year search, Morris II was found. He was crabby-looking but gentle, just like the first Morris. And just like the first Morris, he was whisked away from an animal shelter to fame and fortune.

When Cats Lie, They Tell the Truth About the Temperature

A man named Grinsin once did a study of cats' sleeping places. He measured the temperatures of these places, and he made notes about how the cats were lying as they slept. He found out some very interesting things. See what you can find out.

Things You'll Need:

a room thermometer

notebook and pencil

a cat that you can watch during its naps for several weeks

1. Wait until the cat has gone to sleep. Watch it for a little while. Make notes or make a drawing to show the cat's position when it's asleep.
2. Use a room thermometer to find the air temperature in the spot where the cat is sleeping. (This has to be a thermometer you can carry around with you, because all rooms have warm and cold spots in them.)
3. For a couple of weeks, watch where the cat has its naps. Take the temperature there and make notes or drawings about the cat's position.
4. Do you see any connection between the temperature and the cat's sleeping positions?

Mr. Grinsin found that, in the coldest sleeping spots, cats curl their bodies around in a circle. Their heads and paws are tucked against their tummies, and their tails are wrapped around their bodies. When the temperature is warmer, cats gradually uncurl to a three-quarter circle, and then to a half-circle. When cats sleep in a very warm place, they stretch right out. (To see all these different sleeping positions, you might have to look at more than one cat, and in more than one season of the year.)

By the way, does *your* sleeping position change when the temperature changes? Do you curl up in a ball on a cold night, and lie with your arms and legs stretched out wide on a hot night?

The Whole Kitten Caboodle

Today you're going to bring your new kitten home. Is your home ready for the newcomer? The main thing to remember is that a kitten is not just a small-sized cat, it's a *baby* cat. Your family has to make your home safe for this furry baby, just as you would for a human infant.

Put household chemicals like soaps and cleansers into a cupboard the kitten can't get into, so it won't be poisoned by licking the containers. Check with a veterinarian or at the library to find out whether your houseplants are harmful to cats. Many common plants, including philodendron and ivy, can poison a cat who nibbles the leaves. Curious kittens can fall into toilets and drown, so keep the lids down in your bathrooms.

Here are a few things you need to have ready for your kitten:

1. **Shallow dishes** for milk, water, and food. You might also like to put an old placemat or tea tray under the dishes to catch spills.

2. **Cat food**. (See page 76 to find out what to feed your cat.) A kitten under four months old will need to eat four or five small meals a day. For kittens four months to one year old, two or three feedings is about right.

3. **A litter box and a bag of cat litter**. Put 5 to 7 cm (2 to 3 ins.) of cat litter in a metal or plastic pan. This will be your kitten's toilet. Pet stores sell plastic pans especially for this purpose. A cardboard or wooden box won't do, because it will quickly become soaked and smelly. This will disgust your family, and your cat will refuse to use the box. You also need a slotted spoon to lift solid droppings out of the litter so you can flush them down the toilet.

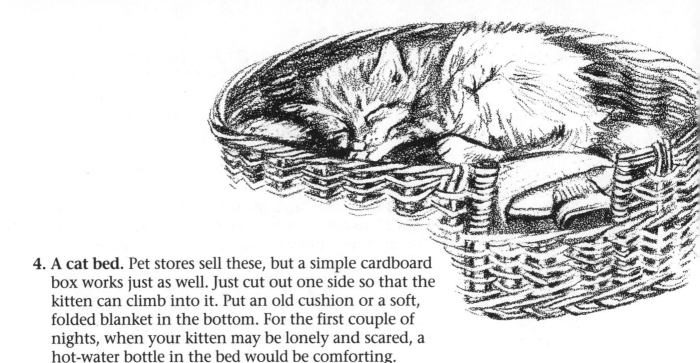

4. **A cat bed.** Pet stores sell these, but a simple cardboard box works just as well. Just cut out one side so that the kitten can climb into it. Put an old cushion or a soft, folded blanket in the bottom. For the first couple of nights, when your kitten may be lonely and scared, a hot-water bottle in the bed would be comforting.

5. **An elasticized (stretchy) collar.** A stretchy collar is important so that your kitten won't choke if its collar gets caught on something. Attach an identification tag to the collar right away.

6. **A fine-toothed metal comb.** This is for grooming your kitten's fur. It is especially important if you have a long-haired cat.

7. **A scratching post.** It's natural for cats to sharpen their claws on things. If you don't give a kitten a post, it may rip up the furniture or carpets. You can make a scratching post by covering a wooden post with an old piece of carpet or by simply attaching a piece of carpet to the wall. Every time you see the kitten start to scratch something, take it to the post and move its front paws back and forth on the material.

SURPRISING FACTS ABOUT CATS

A Litter Bit of Luck

In 1989, the American Veterinary Medical Association gave a special award to Ed Lowe, an inventor who has made cats' lives happier and healthier. Guess what he invented? It wasn't a better brand of cat food, or a catnip mouse, or a flea collar. It was Kitty Litter! If you have a cat, you probably have Mr. Lowe's invention in your house. Kitty Litter — and other brands of cat litter — gives cats a handy indoor toilet.

Before the 1950s, people tried using boxes of dirt, ashes or sawdust for their cats. After one or two cat visits, though, these boxes became very unpleasant to have around. Most people sent their cats outside for the night rather than have smelly boxes in their houses. Mr. Lowe's litter, which controls wetness and odor for days, made it possible for cats to stay inside, warm, dry and safe. Lucky cats. (And lucky Mr. Lowe, who has made millions of dollars from his invention!)

Where will you put your kitten's bed, food, and toilet? There are only two rules about this. First, keep the litter box away from the bed and food. Cats don't like to eat and sleep next to their toilets. Second, put the bed in a quiet spot. Kittens may not get enough rest if their bed is in a busy part of the house.

When you bring your kitten home, don't carry it in your arms. It may be so nervous that it will claw you and wriggle right out of your grasp. Use a cat carrier of some kind, even if it's only a cardboard box with airholes cut into it.

Everyone in the family is going to be excited about the new kitten. Just remember that your wonderful new pet is a living animal, not a toy. There will be plenty of time for cuddling and playing in the coming weeks. Right now, your kitten is bewildered. Don't handle it too much. Give it a chance to look around. After a couple of hours, if it seems calm, you can give it something to eat and drink. Right afterwards, take it to the litter box. Gently scratch its front paws in the litter. Wait until it goes. (Most kittens catch on very quickly, especially if their mother has already shown them what to do.)

Speak softly to your new pet, using its name a lot. Before long, your kitten will feel like one of the family.

Catnip Toys

Did you know that many store-bought "catnip" toys just contain wood chips that have been sprayed with a chemical smelling like catnip? You can make a real catnip toy to delight your favorite cat.

1. Instant Toy

You'll Need:

a baby's or small child's sock with a tight weave so the catnip won't leak through (an adult sock makes a toy too big for a cat to handle)

dried catnip — grow your own or buy a box of catnip in a pet store

string

1. Fill the foot of the sock with dried catnip. Twist the leg of the sock around on itself and tie it in a tight knot. Ta-dah! — a cat toy! (If the leg of the sock is too short to tie, run a line of small stitches across the ankle to close off the sock foot.)
2. If you like, you can tie a piece of string around the knot so that you can drag the toy along the floor. If the cat is going to play with the toy by itself, though, *don't* add the string. Cats can swallow long pieces of string, which may make them very sick.

2. Mouse Toy

If you want to go to a little more trouble, you can make a toy that looks like a mouse.

You'll Need:

a piece of cotton cloth about 15 cm x 30 cm (6 inches x 12 inches) (an old cloth diaper would make a great white mouse!)

pins or tape

needle and thread, or a sewing machine

a small piece of felt

a piece of string about 8 cm (3 inches) long

laundry marking pen

1. Fold the piece of cloth in half, and pin it or tape it to hold it in place. (If you use pins, don't leave any lying around. They're very dangerous for curious cats or babies, who might swallow them.)
2. Draw a mouse shape, like the one in the drawing, on one side of the folded cloth. Cut through both layers of cloth when you cut out your mouse shape. Now you have two mouse shapes exactly the same.

63

3. Pin or tape the two mouse pieces together to hold them while you sew. Start sewing near where the tail will go. Put your line of stitches about 1 cm (1/4 inch) from the edge of the cloth. Make small stitches with no space in between, so that the catnip won't leak out. STOP when you still have about 3 cm (1 inch) to go till you reach your starting point.

4. Turn the mouse inside out, so that its sewn edge is neat and smooth.

5. Fill the mouse with dried catnip. Place the string tail so that about 1.5 cm (1/2 inch) is inside the mouse. Finish stitching the mouse, making sure the tail is held by your stitches.

6. Cut out two felt ears. Stitch them to the two sides of your mouse's head.

7. Give the mouse two eyes (and maybe some whiskers) with a laundry marking pen.

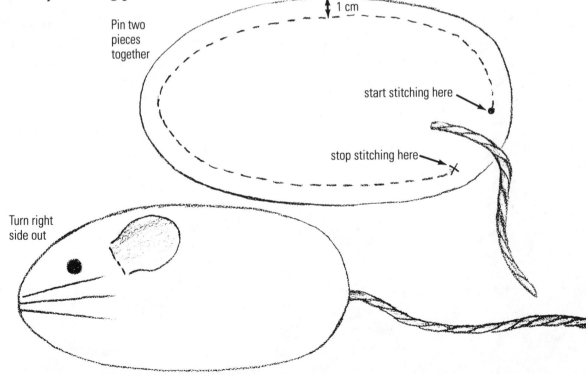

Pin two pieces together

1 cm

start stitching here

stop stitching here

Turn right side out

Pussycat, Pussycat, Where Have You Been?

Should pet cats be kept indoors all the time? Or should they be allowed to run freely outside? People often have very strong feelings about this. Many cat owners like the idea that their cat is outside having an adventurous life of its own. An outdoor cat can explore, hunt mice, and meet other cats.

Other people like to keep their cats safe inside. They know that indoor cats have a much better chance of living to old age. Indoor cats have fewer accidents and get sick less often. Kind owners give their cats toys to play with and don't leave them alone for hours on end. These people often have more than one cat, so that the animals have each other for company.

Most veterinarians and animal welfare societies advise people to keep their cats indoors. This is because they see the bad side of outdoor cat life. They see all the lost cats, and they know that only about three out of every hundred lost cats who are brought to a shelter will be reunited with their families. They also see the cats who are killed or injured. Can you believe that over *one million* dogs and cats are killed by cars in North America every year? Many other cats are killed or hurt in falls and fights with other animals. Still others are poisoned by eating garbage or freeze to death in cold weather.

Cats who run free can also be a nuisance for neighbors. Cats hunt and sometimes kill birds, which is very upsetting for people with bird feeders. Cats dig up people's gardens and use children's sandboxes as toilets. Cats yowl loudly at each other in the middle of the night.

If your cat stays inside, there is little chance that it will get lost. But even indoor cats can suddenly rush out of open doors and disappear. This is why all pet cats should wear a collar and a tag with their family's name and phone number on it. You should also take a good clear photo of your cat.

If the bad day ever comes when your cat is lost, swing into action right away. Tell all the people you know in your neighborhood that your cat is missing. Ask them to check their back yards and especially their garages. In bad weather, cats seek shelter in garages and sometimes get locked in. Call your local animal shelter to find out if your cat has been taken there. Be ready to give the shelter a full description of your cat: its sex, age, color, markings, and anything else that makes your cat easy to spot. For instance, does your cat have a nick in one ear? A very thick tail with rings around it?

Make a poster like the one on page 67. Post copies of it at least five blocks in all directions from where your cat was lost. Check the lost and found column in the newspaper to see if your cat is there. If a few days go by with no word of your pet, ask your parents to run an ad in that column. In the meantime, keep looking. Lost pets sometimes turn up again weeks or months after they disappeared.

Safety Note: Suppose a stranger calls to say your cat has been found. *Do not* invite this person to come to your house unless an adult can be there with you when the person arrives. And *never* go to a stranger's house unless an adult goes with you.

LOST

Have you seen Muffin?

Muffin was last seen September 18 near
Maple Avenue and Orchard Blvd.

DESCRIPTION:
6-month-old female
black with white spot under chin,
yellow eyes

Wt. 2 kg (6 lbs.)

Wearing Humane Society I.D. Tag # B6431

If you find Muffin, please call 333-0000, after 5:00 p.m.

Incredible Journeys

Sugar was a cream-colored part-Persian cat who didn't like car travel. When her family had to make a long move from Anderson, California to Gage, Oklahoma, they decided to leave Sugar behind with a neighbor. Nobody asked Sugar what *she* thought of the plan. Soon after her family left Anderson, Sugar disappeared.

Fourteen months later, in Gage, Oklahoma, Sugar's original owners found her sitting at their front door. How could she make a journey of 2400 km (1500 miles) to a place where she had never been before?

We know that if we had no maps and couldn't ask directions, we could never do what Sugar did. In fact, many people feel that stories like Sugar's can't be true. Maybe, they say, the owners saw a cat that looked like their old cat and wanted to believe it was the same cat. This might happen sometimes, but Sugar had been born with a badly formed hipbone, so her family could be fairly sure they had their own cat back again. Unless we think that people make up stories about their pets, we have to believe that sometimes — very rarely — cats make incredible journeys we can't explain. What do you think?

Infopet to the Rescue

Suppose you find a thin, frightened cat huddled on your porch, meowing for food. You know it's lost, but how do you find out where it lives? Often, lost pets have no collars or tags to tell you. And even when lost pets are taken to animal shelters, many are never reclaimed by their families.

Now there's a new system — Infopet — that helps lost pets and their owners find each other. The Infopet system is already being used by hundreds of veterinarians and animal shelters in the United States and Canada.

A veterinarian can inject a pet with a tiny microchip, about the size of a grain of rice. This just takes a second. Once the chip is in place under the pet's skin, it doesn't show and it doesn't hurt. There is a special 10-digit code on the microchip that identifies the pet and its owners. If this pet ever gets lost, veterinarians and humane societies who use Infopet can read the chip with a special scanner. Then they phone the owners to let them know their pet has been found.

Cat Chat

Even though cats can't speak to us in human languages, they can "talk" to us very well. Cats don't just use their voices, they use their whole bodies to send us messages. When cats arch their backs, lay their ears back and hiss, we know they're very upset. If we try to pick them up, they may scratch us. When cats sit on our laps, purring with their eyes half-closed, we know they're happy and relaxed.

Cats, like human beings, have a need to communicate. *Communication* means letting others know what you're thinking and feeling. Most people communicate by using their voices to speak. (People who can't speak clearly or hear well may communicate in other ways. They may use sign language or point to words on a computer screen.)

When we speak, it's not just the words we use that send our messages. The way we say words — which is called *tone* — is important, too. For instance, when you ask, "What are you doing?" your tone will show whether you are curious, or angry, or frightened.

Cats don't have the right muscles in their lips and tongues to form all the words we can say. Still, they can make a lot of interesting sounds. Mildred Moelk, who studied cat sounds very carefully, reported that cats can say *a*, *e*, *i*, and *u*, as well as the *ow* sound in "meow." She also heard cats making the sounds of *f*, *g*, *k*, *h*, *m*, *n*, *ng* (the sound at the end of "rung"), *r*, *t*, and *w*. Listen closely to your cat. Can you hear these sounds? Do you think you hear any that Mildred Moelk missed?

You could try keeping a list of your cat's sounds. You'll probably find it hard, sometimes, to know what you should write down to show the sound. For instance, most cats make a friendly trilling sound with their lips closed. Mother cats use it to call their kittens. Many cats use it to greet their human friends or to thank someone who has just served their dinner. Mildred Moelk wrote this sound as *mhrn*. If you've heard your cat trill, you'll know what this means. But if you haven't, the letters might not help you very much.

It's easier to write the other sound that cats make to their people: "meow." Cats can say this in many different tones. A loud meow, repeated over and over, might mean, "Get up and feed me breakfast." Another meow, lifting at the end like a question, might mean, "Can I go out?" There are sad meows, frightened meows, and happy meows. Pet owners soon learn to understand their own cat's meow talk.

Because human beings use language so well, we sometimes forget there are other ways of communicating. People can also show their feelings with no words at all. They can clench their fists and narrow their eyes when they're angry. They can jump up and down when they're excited. This is called *body language*.

Cats express many things with their body language. You probably already know that a cat switches its tail back and forth quickly when it's angry. But do you know that there are many other cat-tail messages? When a cat's tail curves down and then up again at the tip, the cat is feeling peaceful and relaxed. When its tail is straight up and the hairs are standing straight out from it like a brush, the cat is angry or frightened and may attack.

Tail talk is sometimes mixed with other body language. For instance, a cat who feels threatened by a dog stretches its legs to stand tall. At the same time, it arches its back in an upside down"U" shape, and a ridge of fur stands up stiffly along its spine and tail. The cat is trying to look as big and fierce as possible, so that the dog will think twice about coming closer.

Although we can use our whole bodies to show feelings, we usually show them most in our faces. Cats have very expressive faces, too. Their eyes, their ears, and even their whiskers can send all kinds of different messages. A happy cat holds its ears upright and relaxes its whiskers. An angry cat turns its ears backwards and points them up. Its pupils (the black part of the eye) close down to narrow slits and its whiskers bristle forward. A frightened cat opens its pupils wide and lays its ears flat against its head. Its whiskers, too, are pulled back against its face. Both angry and frightened cats will hiss and even spit.

People who study animal behavior have come up with an interesting idea about why cats hiss. An angry, hissing cat, with its ears laid flat, its pupils squeezed into slits, and its jaws opened wide to hiss ,

looks and sounds like a poisonous snake. Enemies are so startled they stop in their tracks, giving the cat time to flee. This is called *protective mimicry*. It means looking like something more dangerous than you are, so that other animals won't attack you.

Sometimes people don't quite understand the messages cats send them. For instance, you arrive home and your cat pushes the side of its head against your leg. Then it rubs the whole side of its body against you, and finishes up by half-twining its tail around you. Is this a friendly greeting? Yes, but it's more than

that. Your cat is marking you as its property! Cats have special scent glands at the corners of their mouths, on the sides of their heads, and near the base of their tails. When your cat rubs against you, it puts its scent on you. You can't smell it, but your cat and other cats can. When it rubs against you, your cat also picks up your scent. If your cat goes and has a wash after rubbing against you, it's having a friendly, reassuring taste of you!

Suppose you are sitting with your cat on your lap. You're stroking the cat and it's purring peacefully. Then it begins to dig its claws into your knees, first one paw, then the other. This can be quite uncomfortable. Why would your cat do this? Baby kittens, drinking from their mother's nipples, knead her tummy with their paws to get the milk flowing. So when your cat kneads you, it's feeling just as contented and safe as a kitten with its mother.

Surprising Facts About Cats

Where's the Purr?

Have you ever wondered how a cat purrs? You might be surprised to know that people who study cats don't agree on the answer.

Most cat experts seem to think that cats purr with their "false" vocal cords. Like you, a cat has vocal cords in its throat. When air passes over these cords and makes them vibrate (shake back and forth very fast), you and your cat can make sounds. (Do you make sounds on the in-breath or the out-breath? Try it and see.) However, a cat has an extra pair of cords in its throat. When air passes over these, on the in-breath *and* on the out-breath, it probably makes the rhythmic rumbling sound of a purr.

Some people think that a cat's purr doesn't come from its throat at all. Instead, they think that a purr is the sound of blood rushing through the big blood vessels in a cat's chest. Listen carefully the next time your cat purrs. If your cat is feeling very relaxed, you might be able to put your ear to its throat and chest. Where do *you* think the sound is coming from?

Do You Read Me?

Cats send messages with their eyes, with their ears, with their tails — in fact, with their whole bodies. How good are you at sending messages without talking?

Things You'll Need:
a friend to try this with

14 small cards or pieces of paper

a pencil

a scarf

1. Write these seven words on seven cards, one word per card: Happy, Surprised, Scared, Sad, Angry, Disgusted, Bored. Then make another set of seven cards with the same words.
2. Give one set of cards to your friend. Give your friend a chance to look through the cards. Meanwhile, shuffle your cards so that you won't know what order they're in.
3. Sit facing your friend. Turn up a card without letting your friend see it. Try to show the feeling written on the card, just by using your face. Don't make any sounds at all. Can your friend guess what mood you are trying to express?
4. Take turns trying this out. Which feelings are the hardest ones to show? Which are the easiest?

5. Now tie a scarf loosely around your head so that your friend can't see your face. Try to show one of the feelings on the cards with your body. How do you hold your arms and hands when you're mad? How do you stand when you're sad? Take turns with your friend.

6. Is it easier to show feelings when you can just use your face or when you can use everything but your face?

In everyday life, try to pay more attention to what people are saying to you, not just with words, but also with their faces and bodies. You'll be amazed at how much better you can understand people's feelings.

Bright-Eyed and Bushy-Tailed

If big cans of dog food are on sale at the supermarket, can you buy them for your cat? No! Cats and dogs need very different foods. Cats can't stay healthy on a diet of people's table scraps, either. Dogs —and people— are *omnivores* (everything-eaters). Cats are true *carnivores* (meat-eaters). They need much more protein and fat in their food than dogs and people do.

Cats also need a chemical called *taurine*. Most mammals are able to make this chemical inside their own bodies, but cats can't, and without it they go blind. If they were wild-cats, they would get it from the bodies of their prey. Most cat food — but not dog food— has taurine added to it.

How can you tell if a certain brand of cat food is healthy for your pet? The Canadian Veterinary Medical Association (CVMA) has set up a group to test cat foods. They put their seal on the can or package of any food that meets their standards. Give your cat lots of different kinds and flavors of cat food to make sure it gets a balanced diet. Cats will get sick if they eat only tuna or only liver. Read the cat food label to find out how much to feed your cat. As you might expect, bigger cats and active cats need more food than smaller cats and cats who like to lie around.

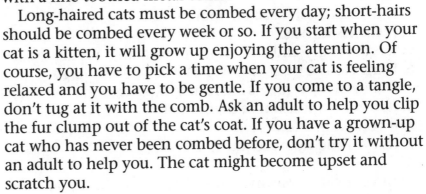

Cats shouldn't be given food right from the refrigerator. It chills their small bodies too much. Heat it by adding a little warm water or let it sit out of the refrigerator for a little while before you serve it. Cats should also have a dish of water they can drink whenever they want to. Kittens like milk, but adult cats don't need it; in fact, milk upsets the stomachs of some cats.

Cats, unlike dogs, hardly ever need baths. Most cats do a good job of keeping themselves clean with their rough tongues. But, while they're grooming themselves, they swallow some of their fur. Too much swallowed fur can make them sick, so help your cat out by combing its fur with a fine-toothed metal comb.

Long-haired cats must be combed every day; short-hairs should be combed every week or so. If you start when your cat is a kitten, it will grow up enjoying the attention. Of course, you have to pick a time when your cat is feeling relaxed and you have to be gentle. If you come to a tangle, don't tug at it with the comb. Ask an adult to help you clip the fur clump out of the cat's coat. If you have a grown-up cat who has never been combed before, don't try it without an adult to help you. The cat might become upset and scratch you.

Your family should make sure your cat gets its *vaccinations* (shots). Vaccinations protect your cat from diseases that could kill it, such as distemper and feline respiratory disease (which is like a *very* bad cold). A veterinarian will usually start to give a kitten its shots when it is about eight weeks old.

Your cat should also see a veterinarian if it seems sick. According to the Toronto Humane Society, here are some things to watch for:

1. Your cat won't eat for several days
2. It vomits (throws up) with a lot of force, or again and again
3. It doesn't wash itself anymore
4. It shakes its head or scratches its ears
5. Its coat is dry and dull, or its fur is falling out in patches
6. It tries to use its litter box, but it can't seem to go
7. Its bowel movements are runny, bloody, or discolored
8. It urinates (pees) more than usual
9. It coughs or sneezes a lot
10. Its eyes and nose are runny

When your cat is showing any of these symptoms, take it to a vet right away. If you want your pet to live a long and healthy life, a veterinarian is your cat's best friend.

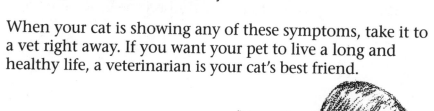

Fast Feline Feast

You can prepare this special treat in a couple of minutes — and your cat will love you for it.

Things You'll Need:
your cat's food dish

a stirring spoon

Ingredients
dry cat food

juice saved from a 184 g (6-1/2 oz.) can of water-packed tuna

a little minced parsley ("minced" means chopped in tiny bits)

What to Do:
1. Put a serving of dry food in your cat's bowl.
2. Pour a little tuna juice over the dry food. The food should be moist but not soggy.
3. Add a sprinkle of minced parsley.
4. Mix everything together quickly with the spoon. Serve it right away.

❧ Try it Yourself

Moggie's Munchies

"Moggie" is what many people in England say instead of "pussycat" or "kitty." Moggie is also the name of a cat I know who looks forward to mealtimes — and loves these special, homemade treats.

Things You'll Need:

a saucepan

a measuring cup

measuring spoons

a stirring spoon

a cookie sheet

oven mitts

a frypan

a slotted spoon

paper towels

an airtight container to store the munchies

Ingredients

250 mL (1 cup) of brown rice

500 mL (2 cups) of beef or chicken broth (you can make this or buy it in cans at the grocery store)

30 to 45 mL (2 to 3 tbsp.) of cooking oil

THE WELL-FED PUSSYCAT

Once upon a time, cats caught their own meals of mice and birds. Now that we're providing most of their food, what should we be putting in their dishes? How can we tell if the cat food we're buying is the right one for our pet? Why can't cats be vegetarians? Do cats need vitamin pills? The Canadian Veterinary Medical Association has a free booklet that answers all these questions.

Write to:
The CVMA Food Certification Program
339 Booth Street
Ottawa, Ontario
K1R 7K1

Ask for: A Commonsense Guide to Feeding Your Dog and Cat

Don't forget: Print your own address clearly on your letter, so that they'll know where to send your booklet.

Ask permission before you use the stove and the oven. If you are not allowed to cook things on your own, ask an adult to help you.

1. Pour the broth into the saucepan. Heat it on medium-high heat until it boils. (The soup is boiling when it's rolling and bubbling.)
2. Stir in the rice. When the broth mixture starts boiling again, turn the heat down to low. Put a lid on the saucepan and let it simmer for about 40 minutes. ("Simmer" means that the soup is steaming and moving a little, but not bubbling hard as it does when it boils.)
3. Stir the rice every 10 minutes or so to make sure it isn't sticking to the bottom. After 40 minutes, all the broth should be soaked up by the rice.
4. Heat the oven to 200°C (400°F). Spread the cooked rice on a cookie sheet. Bake it in the oven for about 20 minutes, until the rice is brown and crackly. Put on oven mitts and take the cookie sheet out of the oven. Turn off the oven.
5. *Be sure an adult is standing by for this step!* Heat the oil in the frypan over medium heat. Add the rice to the pan about 125 mL (1/2 cup) at a time. Shake the pan a little until the rice becomes puffy.
6. Use a slotted spoon to take the rice out of the frypan. Put the rice on a paper towel to soak up the oil.
7. Keep going until all the rice is puffed up and spread on the paper towels. *When the munchies are cool*, you can feed some to your cat. Put the leftovers in an airtight container.

Traveling Time

Early one summer morning, the Emorys loaded their suitcases into the car and set off on their vacation. Samantha sat in the back seat, holding their new kitten, Clyde. Beside her sat her younger brother, Michael. Samantha had promised Michael that after lunch he could hold Clyde. As soon as the car pulled out of the driveway, though, Samantha felt Clyde begin to tremble.

By the time the Emorys turned onto the highway, Clyde had squirmed free of Samantha's grasp. He was trying to squeeze himself under the seat in front of her. When Michael tried to pull him out, Clyde panicked. He scrambled up over the front seat, bounced off a map that Mrs. Emory was reading, and landed on Mr. Emory's shoulder. Clyde dug in with all his little needle claws. Mr. Emory swerved wildly before he could bring the car to a safe stop at the side of the road.

Wriggling and yowling, Clyde was driven back home, wrapped tightly in a car blanket. He was left behind with a cat-loving neighbor. The Emorys decided they'd made a big mistake in trying to take a cat with them on vacation.

The following summer, the Emorys decided to try again to take Clyde along on their holiday. They followed their veterinarian's advice about how to keep Clyde happy on the highway. Clyde rode on the seat between Michael and Samantha in his own cat carrier. This was the same carrier the Emorys used when they took Clyde to the vet, so he was already used to it. The soft blanket from his cat bed was spread on the bottom.

Whenever the Emorys stopped for a break, they gave Clyde a drink of water and offered him some cat food. (They used the kind that comes in a foil pouch, because it's easiest to pack and doesn't spoil in the summer heat.) If they stopped to go to the bathroom, they gave Clyde a chance to go, too. (They had brought along his litter pan with litter in it, all wrapped up in a plastic garbage bag.) Before the Emorys opened the car door, they put a harness on Clyde and attached a leash to it. That way they could take him for a little exercise without worrying that he might run away in a strange place.

Most cats can learn to travel in a car, just as Clyde did. Here are some other things to remember when you take your cat along for the ride:

1. Before you go, make sure your cat has had all the shots it needs. If you'll be crossing the border into the United States, carry proof that your cat has had its rabies shot.

2. Make sure your cat is wearing a collar and a tag with your home address and phone number. If you will be staying in one main place on your holiday, put your holiday address and phone number on the tag, too.

3. Some cats are very nervous travelers, especially the first day of a trip. Some get carsick and may even throw up. Your vet may be able to prescribe some medicine to help calm your cat . Ask your vet whether your cat should fast (go without food) for a few hours before your trip.

4. *Never* leave your cat in a parked car in warm weather. Even if the car is parked in the shade, the temperature inside can rise very quickly. (And shady patches can disappear as the sun moves across the sky.)

5. If you're going to be staying in hotels, check ahead to find out whether they will accept cats.

6. If everyone's going out and your cat will be in the hotel room alone, put the cat in the bathroom. (Give it a litter box, some water, and a soft cushion or blanket to lie on, of course.) Why? Even a well-behaved cat may use the rug as a bathroom or claw the furniture if it's bored or upset. If your cat makes a mess of the room, the hotel may not let pets stay there anymore.

SOMETHING TO SEND FOR

IS CAMPING FOR CATS?

Wow! Your family is going camping for two whole weeks! You can hardly wait. Will your cat have a good time, too? It won't if it gets lost in the bush or runs into a porcupine. But if you leave it behind, will it be well cared for? The Toronto Humane Society has a leaflet that explains how to give your pet a safe and happy holiday, whether you take it along or leave it at home.

Write to:
Toronto Humane Society
11 River Street
Toronto, Ontario
M5A 4C2

Ask for: Holidays and Pets

Cost: 50¢ **plus** a long envelope with a stamp and your address on it. (Fold this envelope and put it inside the envelope you send to the humane society. They will use this envelope to send the leaflet to you.)

Training — And Airplaning — Your Cat

Can you take your cat on a train or an airplane? At the time I was writing this book, only seeing eye dogs (and hearing ear dogs for the deaf) were allowed on Amtrak, the American passenger rail service. However, you can take your cat on VIA Rail in Canada. The cat must be in a carrier cage, which is put in the baggage car. The owner can go to the baggage car to feed the animal and give it water when the train makes a stop.

Every airline has different rules, so it's important to check with them about pets before booking a flight. Air Canada, for instance, allows pets only in its baggage hold. The animal must be in a sturdy cage, and it must have food and water with it. It won't be allowed out of the cage until its owners pick it up at the end of the trip. The cat must have a certificate of health from a veterinarian and proof that it has had a rabies shot. Some airlines — American Airlines, for one — allow pets in the cabin with the passengers, if they are small enough to be in a cage that fits under the seat. The pet needs the same health certificates that Air Canada asks for.

It might seem like fun to take your pet along on a trip. But your family should think carefully about it. Very nervous cats, cats with health problems, and old cats may suffer on long trips. It might be wiser to leave your pet behind with a kind caregiver.

Kitty in the Clouds

Felix, a two-year-old Calico, may hold the cat record for long-distance flying. Somehow, she escaped from her traveling box in the cargo hold of a 747 flying from West Germany to Los Angeles. When the plane landed, she was nowhere to be found.

The plane carried on with its scheduled flights, and Felix went along for the ride. She traveled more than 288,000 km (almost 180,000 miles) and made 64 stops before she was recaptured by airline employees. On her flight home, Felix finally traveled first class. She dined on tuna, steak and caviar, and slept contentedly on the lap of a flight attendant.

Old Friends

Suppose someone showed you pictures of a 60-year-old person and a 25-year-old person. You'd have no trouble telling which person is older, would you? But if someone showed you pictures of two-year-old Tiger and 10-year-old Smoky, you probably couldn't pick out the older cat. Unlike people, cats don't change their looks much as they age. Some cats get a sprinkling of white hairs in their black fur. Some cats grow a little fatter, while other cats become thinner. Because these aren't big or sudden changes, it's easy to forget that the years are catching up with our pets.

People sometimes say that one year in the life of a cat is the same as seven years of human life. This doesn't quite work out, though. Some one-year-old female cats are already having kittens. And quite a few cats live to be 18 or 20. By this counting system, they'd be about 130 person-years old! People who have studied cats' lifespans say that a one-year-old cat is about the same as a 15-year-old human being. When a cat is two, it's like a 25-year-old. When it's 10, it's like a 60-year-old person, and when it's 20, it's as old as a person who is 90.

If you are 10 years old and your cat is also 10, it might be hard for you to realize that your pet is getting old. You might sometimes be unkind to your cat without meaning to be. If you're playing with your cat, don't tease it or chase it until it's exhausted. Let the old-timer set the pace. I knew a 17-year-old cat who still liked to play with a piece of string, but she only played by her rules. She would roll over on her back and bat at the string when it brushed her paw. If it was just a little farther away, she ignored it.

If you notice your older cat having a nap, don't wake it up. It needs the extra rest time. All cats need warmth, but old cats need it even more. They may feel stiff and sore sometimes, and a sunny windowsill is very comforting. Make sure your "senior catizen" has a warm place to sleep, sheltered from drafts.

When they are feeling stiff, older cats may skip some of their grooming. If your cat's fur is getting tangled, give it some help with a grooming comb. Sometimes old cats lose their sense of taste and smell, so they don't enjoy their food as much. Give them special food treats from time to time. On the other hand, don't overfeed your cat. Older cats are less active, so they need less food than they did when they were younger. Being overweight can lead to health problems.

Regular visits to the veterinarian are a good idea for any cat, but especially for older ones. Thirty years ago, cats only lived about 8 or 10 years. Today, with many advances in medical care for cats, they often live to be twice as old as this. It's always sad for cat owners to realize that their pets will grow old and die before they do. On the other hand, it's good to know that cats have the longest lives of all small mammal pets. And with kind care and good food, most cats will stay happy and active even in their old age.

Tubby Tabby

The heaviest cat on record was a male tabby named Himmy. Himmy lived in Australia. In 1986, he weighed a whopping 21.3 kg (46 lbs., 15-1/4 oz.). This is as heavy as many five-year-old children. If a cat as big as Himmy leaped into your arms, he might knock you over !

Ancient Puss

Who was the oldest pet cat ever? Perhaps it was Puss, of Devon, England. Puss was reported to be celebrating his 36th birthday on November 28, 1939. (Some people who study cats accept this record; others say that no cat has ever lived beyond 30.) At any rate, poor old Puss just made it to his record-breaking birthday — he died the next day. Maybe all the fuss on his special day was just too much for him!

Index